THE *Herbal* YEARBOOK

THE *Herbal* YEARBOOK

A celebration of nature's herbs and herbal flowers

LANSDOWNE

THE LANGUAGE OF HERBS & HERBAL FLOWERS

Angelica . . . . *inspiration; magic*

Basil, ornamental . . . . *hatred*

Basil, sweet . . . . . *good wishes; fidelity*

Bay leaf . . . . . . *'I change but in death'*

Bay wreath . . . . *reward of merit*

Borage . . . . *bluntness*

Chamomile . . . . . . *energy in adversity*

Dandelion . . . . *rustic oracle*

Elder . . . . *zealousness*

Fennel . . . *worthy of all praise; strength*

Geranium, lemon . . . *unexpected meeting*

Geranium, rose . . . . *preference*

Hyssop . . . . *cleanliness*

Jasmine . . . . *amiability*

Juniper . . . . *succour; protection*

Lavender . . . . *distrust*

Lemon . . . . *zest*

Lemon blossoms . . . . . *fidelity in love*

Marigold . . . . *grief; despair*

Marjoram . . . . *blushes*

Mint . . . . *virtue*

Nasturtium . . . . *patriotism*

Orange blossom . . . *'Your purity equals your loveliness'*

Parsley . . . . *festivity*

Pennyroyal . . . . *flee away*

Peppermint . . . . *warmth of feeling*

Raspberry . . . . *remorse*

Rose . . . . *love*

Rose, deep red . . . . . . *bashful shame*

Rose, white . . . . . *'I am worthy of you'*

Rosemary . . . . *remembrance*

Rue . . . . *repentance*

Sage . . . . *domestic virtue*

Thyme . . . . *activity or courage*

Violet, blue . . . . *faithfulness*

Violet, sweet . . . . *modesty*

Yarrow . . . . *war*

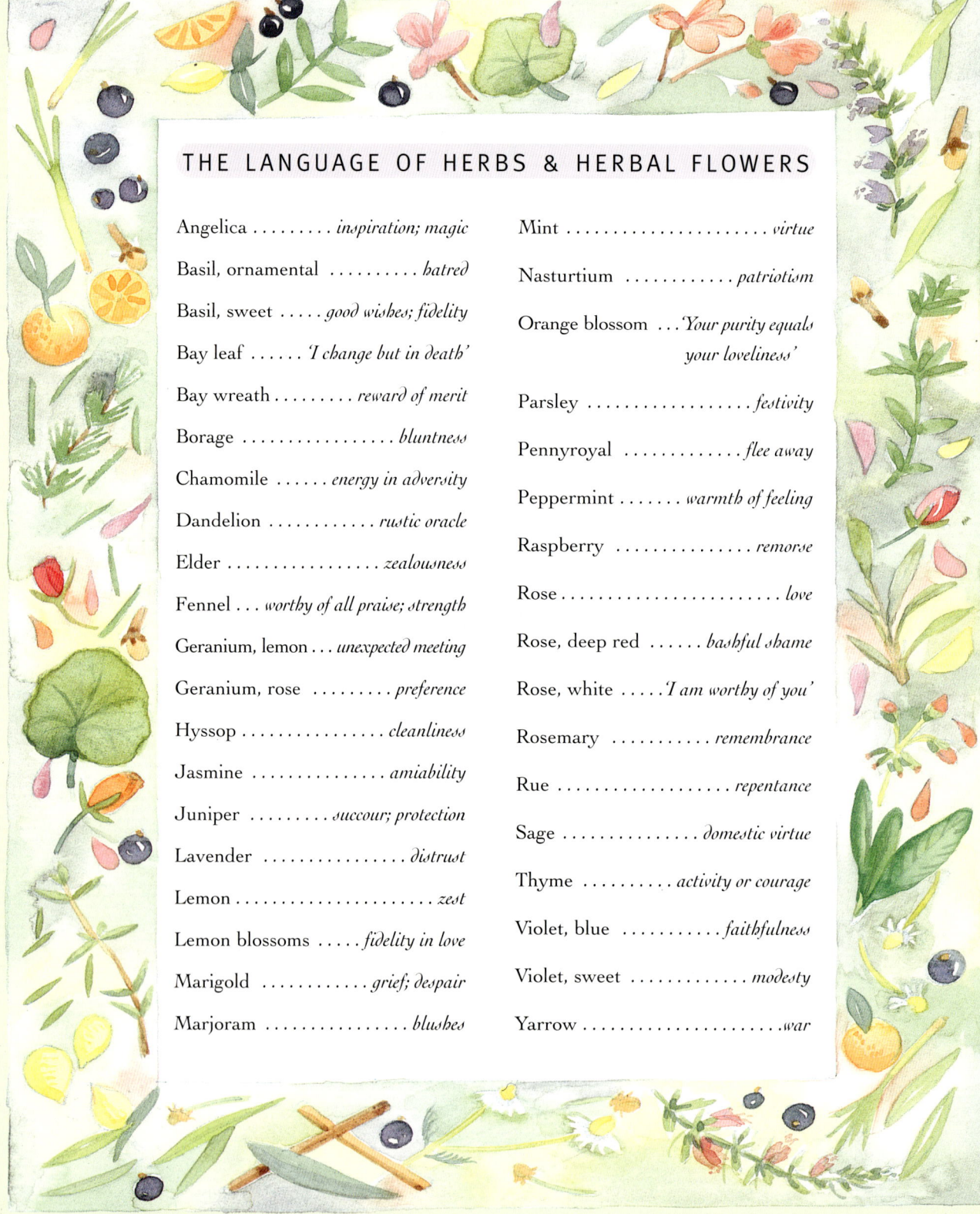

MAGICAL HERBS

HERB	PROPERTIES
Angelica	protects against psychic attack
Basil	gives courage before initiation
Borage	promotes happiness and joy
Chamomile	calms and protects
Chervil	promotes wisdom
Cinnamon	aids concentration and focus
Coriander	brings immortality, peace
Cucumber	increases psychic ability and intuition
Dill	dispels negative energies
Fennel	protects, aids ability to face danger and adversity
Garlic	protects, enhances power of strength
Ginger	protects
Honeysuckle	aids understanding of mysteries
Hyssop	protects, particularly the house
Jasmine	gives psychic protection
Lavender	increases awareness
Parsley	heightens communion with Mother Earth
Peppermint	improves divination skills
Sage	promotes wisdom and cleanses evil
Verbena	enhances lucid dreaming

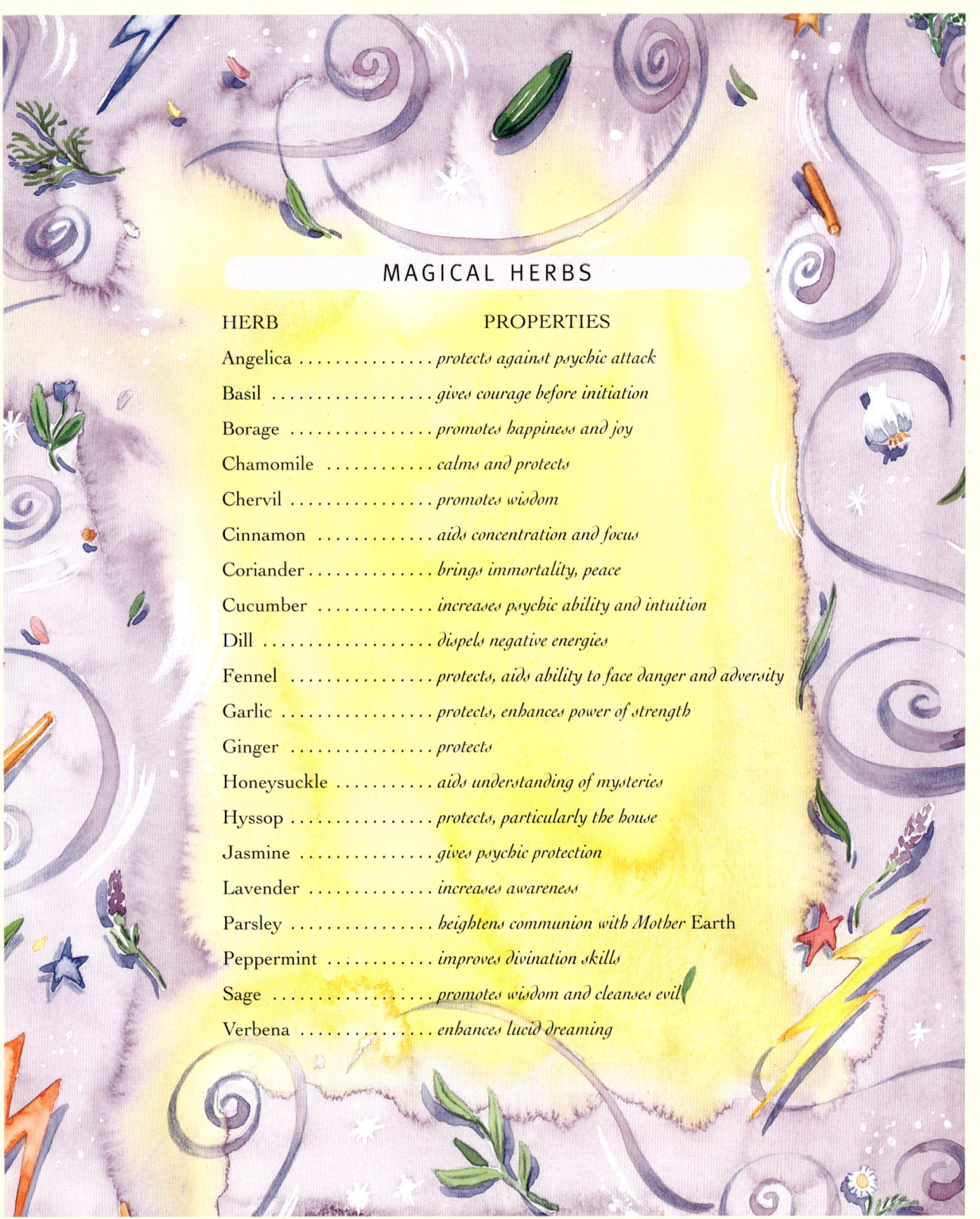

"How could such sweet and wholesome hours be reckon'd but with herbs and flow'rs."

Lavender

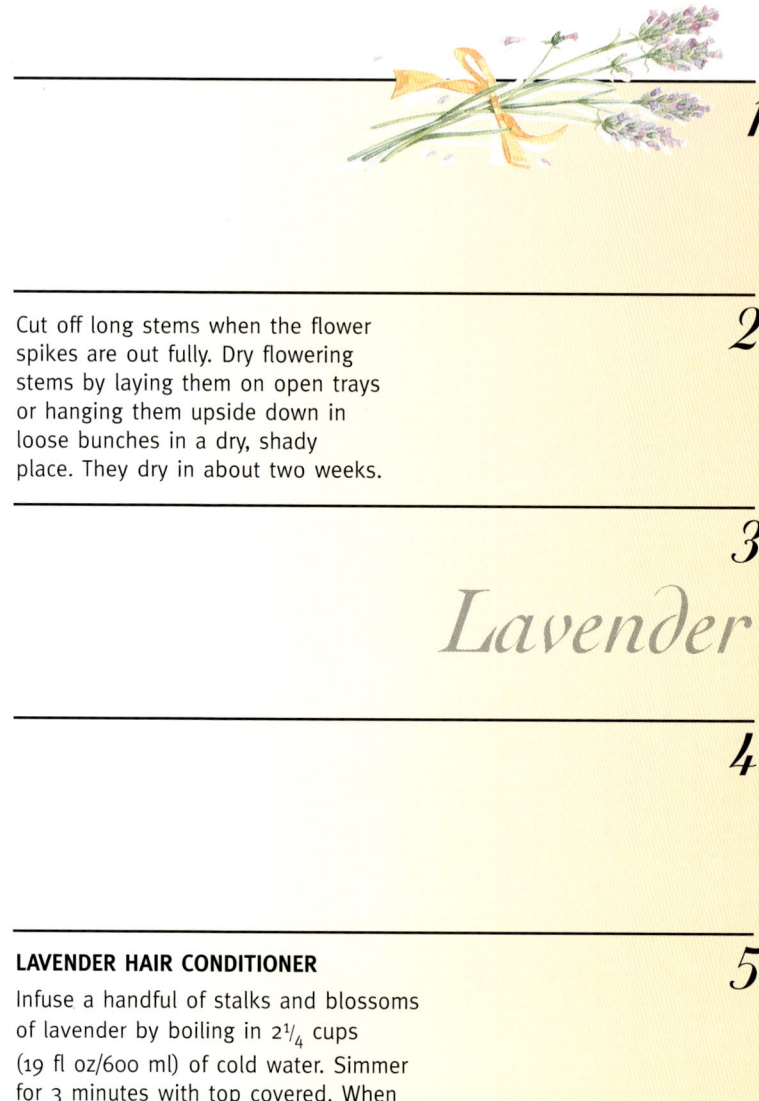

Lavender sachets not only provide a beautiful perfume for drawers and wardrobes, they also protect linen from moths. The sachets are made from dried flowers, crushed and sewn up in muslin. The best time to gather the flowering stems is just as the flowers open. The leaves can be picked at any time.

Culinary uses

- Lavender flowers can be used to flavor jam, honey, sweets, vinegar and tea.
- Mix small amounts with other herbs to create fragrant stews.
- Crystallized lavender makes an attractive decoration for cakes.
- Infused lavender flowers make a tea that reduces anxiety, headaches, nausea and halitosis.

Cut off long stems when the flower spikes are out fully. Dry flowering stems by laying them on open trays or hanging them upside down in loose bunches in a dry, shady place. They dry in about two weeks.

LAVENDER HAIR CONDITIONER
Infuse a handful of stalks and blossoms of lavender by boiling in $2\frac{1}{4}$ cups (19 fl oz/600 ml) of cold water. Simmer for 3 minutes with top covered. When cool, use as a hair conditioner.

JANUARY

8

9

10

11

LAVENDER FLOWER BATH FOAM
This relaxing bath foam is easy to make. Dissolve 12 tbsp grated castile soap in 10 tbsp boiling water, then stir in 4 tbsp crushed dried lavender flowers. Stir until the mixture is well blended. Pour into a bottle, cool, cover and label.

12

LAVENDER WATER
Lavender water can be made easily at home by mixing $\frac{1}{2}$ oz/15 g of lavender oil, $1\frac{1}{4}$ cups (10 fl oz/327 ml) of spirits of wine and a drop of musk in a container.

13

Lavender

14 In Spain, lavender is strewn in churches for its perfume, and Spanish women use essential oil of lavender as a hair lotion.

Medicinal uses
- *Diluted essential lavender oil can be used as an antiseptic and pain killer.*
- *It can be blended for use as a massage oil for coughs, rheumatic and muscular aches, insomnia and depression.*
- *Lavender water is good for oily or spotty skin and helps to speed cell renewal.*

In Elizabethan times, lavender was sewn into dresses and gloves and quilted in a cap. Lavender drops were an ingredient in the smelling salts used to revive swooning women in the 19th century.

15

16

17

18

19

Marigold

20

MARIGOLD-SCENTED SUGAR
Mix some washed and dried petals of marigold flowers with twice their volume of sugar. Spread the mixture on baking trays and place in the oven at the lowest setting for about 2 hours, turning frequently until the sugar has absorbed the moisture from the petals and dried. Cool, sieve and store in a cool, dry place.

21

Marigold

The marigold, also known as calendula, is a colorful flower and a versatile herb. It has been valued for centuries for its cosmetic and culinary uses, as a dye plant and for its healing properties.

The marigold plant prefers sunny positions and grows well in fine loam. However, it tolerates most soils, except when waterlogged. It grows best in cooler seasons. For almost continuous flowers, remove dead flower heads regularly. The marigold is not suitable for growing indoors.

JANUARY

22

> The marigold that goes to bed wi' th' sun
> And with him rises weeping.
> William Shakespeare

23

24

Marigold

25

26

27

28

Culinary uses

- Use the petals to give rice, fish and soup a light, tangy flavor.
- Sprinkle leaves and petals in salads.
- Garnish meat platters and fruit salad with flowers.

Medicinal uses

- Infused oil or cream is good for dry or inflamed skin.
- An infusion stimulates the liver.
- Calendula is antiseptic, antifungal and anti-inflammatory.

Marigold Pudding

Take a pretty quantity of marygold flowers very well shred, mingle with a pint of cream on new milk and almost a pound of beef suet chopt very small, the gratings of a twopenny loaf and stirring all together put it into a bag flower'd and tie it fast. It will be boil'd within an hour — or bake in a pan.

John Evelyn, Acetaria, *1699*

Nasturtium

Nasturtiums belong to the same family as watercress and have the same peppery 'bite'. An annual, self-seeding, creeping and climbing plant, its leaves are round, flat, smooth and pale green, with bright, showy flowers, ranging from pale yellow through to dark red in color. Nasturtiums are easily raised from seed. Plant them in a sunny, frost-free place and water moderately. The soil should not be too rich, as this inhibits the growth of the flowers. They repel beetles and aphis and are good to plant near apple trees, grapes, broccoli and courgette (zucchini). Nasturtiums are attractive and useful plants but they grow rampantly can suffocate and choke nearby plants.

Nasturtium

The spicy 'bite' of the leaves makes an ideal replacement for salt and pepper in cooking. The leaves are rich in vitamin C and are valuable when colds are in force.

The seeds are also useful — they can be pickled and served as a substitute for capers. The leaves may be torn into salads or used in sandwiches, and the flowers add a wonderful touch of color to salads and as garnishes for cold dishes.

NASTURTIUM SALAD
- lettuce leaves
- 6 nasturtium leaves, torn
- 1 cup well-washed and dried young nasturtium flowers
- 1 tbsp finely chopped chervil
- 1 generous sprig of Italian parsley, chopped
- French dressing

Line a glass bowl with well-washed and dried lettuce leaves. Heap the chopped leaves and whole flowers mixed with the chervil and parsley in the centre of the bowl. Pass the dressing separately. Serves 4.

"A merry heart doeth good like a medicine"

Proverbs, Ch 17, v 22

Medicinal Herbs

The benefits of orthodox medicine are undisputed, however, alternative forms of healing and prevention of illness are becoming more widely recognized and accepted. Most alternative forms of healing use herbs during treatment.

Herbs have been used medicinally for thousands of years. The Ancient Egyptians and Greeks were the first people known to write down in technical terms their knowledge of herbs. In the Middle Ages monks cultivated herbs and made many advances in their cultivation and use. It is well known that the first liqueurs were created by monks as potent medicines.

Herbal remedies can offer immediate relief or remedy to conditions that usually have a short duration; ailments such as coughs, colds, and sore throats, for example. For a longstanding or chronic health problem, herbal treatment is best thought of in terms of months rather than weeks and ideally should be monitored by a trained herbalist.

Medicinal

A seed infusion of **FENNEL** relieves bloating and aids digestion. It eases stomach pains when added to laxative mixtures and helps increase nursing mothers' milk flow.

To relieve a heavy cold, grate **HORSERADISH** and inhale the fumes that arise.

FEBRUARY

8

9

10

Herbs

11

12

13

14

Diluted **LAVENDER** oil is antiseptic and painkilling. Blend for use as a massage oil for ticklish coughs, rheumatic and muscular aches, insomnia and depression. To treat a simple household burn, gently pat lavender oil over the sore part. This will take away the pain and will help to heal the skin tissue.

To cure corns, try crushing a **COMFREY** leaf in your hands until it becomes moist, then place over the corn and cover it with an old sock. Apply before going to bed, and repeat over a few nights. The corn will disappear very quickly.

BORAGE has an ancient reputation as a heart tonic; it calms palpitations and revitalizes the system during convalescence. It has a relaxing effect and is said to give courage and help relieve grief and sadness.

Caution: Use the leaves in moderate amounts.

THYME helps digestion and hangovers. Thyme oil is an anti-oxidant and reduces cell ageing, and it is also antiseptic and antifungal. It relieves muscular pain and rheumatism, and stimulates the immune system to fight infection.

Caution: Use oil in low dilutions; avoid during pregnancy.

Medicinal

The best home remedy for gall bladder distress is the addition of fresh **LEMON** or lemon juice and olive oil to meals, especially salads.

To ease bronchitis and tightness of the chest, chop **GARLIC** into small pieces and put into a jar of vaseline. Stand on a warm hob for a few days. When cold, massage freely into back and chest. Garlic can help reduce cholesterol levels in the blood. Adding garlic, especially raw garlic, to the diet may help reduce blood pressure. Garlic and horseradish tablets may reduce hayfever by strengthening the immune system.

15

16

17

18

19

20

21

FEBRUARY

22

23
Herbal ointment containing **RUE** promotes pain relief from arthritis when rubbed into the affected parts of the body for about 30 minutes at least once a day.

24

25
One of the most interesting uses of **TANSY** in the past was as an embalming agent and a meat preservative. Use the whole herb to treat inflammations, cuts, sprains and varicose veins.

Caution: Over-large doses of tansy can be fatal. Do not use internally except with professional advice and under supervision.

26
Herbs

27

28

SAGE is a highly antiseptic herb and is an excellent remedy for colds, fevers and sore throats. Insect bites can be alleviated by rubbing the skin with fresh sage leaves.

Caution: Avoid if you are pregnant or have epilepsy.

The pain of burns, including sunburn, can be relieved by **ALOE VERA**, a great analgesic and healer. Apply aloe vera leaf gel three times daily for about 30 minutes. Once burn wounds have closed, **COMFREY** ointment can help reduce scarring.

Medicinal Herbs

To improve poor circulation contributing to varicose veins, drink a cup of **GINGER** tea three times daily. **CHILLI** and **GINGER** should be added to the diet and **MARIGOLD** ointment massaged into the affected area relieves itchiness and pain.

Caution: Never massage any veins with dark blue lumps.

FEVERFEW taken as tablets, tincture or infusion for a period of a month or so has cleared migraine pain for many people. A fresh leaf may be chewed but it is very bitter and may cause a sore mouth.

ROSEMARY leaves and flowers can be used to heal wounds, cuts, sores, stings and bites. They relieve spasms, induce perspiration and the flow of bile, calm the nerves and stimulate the circulation.

Caution: Do not take rosemary in large doses or over extended periods of time, and never take the oil internally.

"Wel loved he garleek, oynons, and eek lekes,
And for to drynken stron wyn, reed as blood"

Chaucer, The Canterbury Tales

Garlic

Garlic

Garlic enhances savoury dishes worldwide and has important medicinal properties. Garlic belongs to the onion (allium) family and grows well in rich, moist and well-drained soil. It needs sun or partial shade. Garlic bulbs need to be replanted every three or four years.

Plant garlic near roses to enhance rose scent. A bulb is made up of 5 to 20 garlic cloves; its flavor increases the more it is sliced or crushed. Use garlic sparingly to enhance meat, seafood and many vegetable dishes.

This was anciently accounted the poor man's treacle, it being a remedy for all diseases and hurts (except those which itself breeds.) It ... helps the biting of mad dogs, and other venomous creatures ... purges the head, helps the lethargy, is a good preservative against, and a remedy for, any plague, sore, or foul ulcer; takes away spots and blemishes in the skin, eases pains in the ears ...
Nicholas Culpeper, 17th century

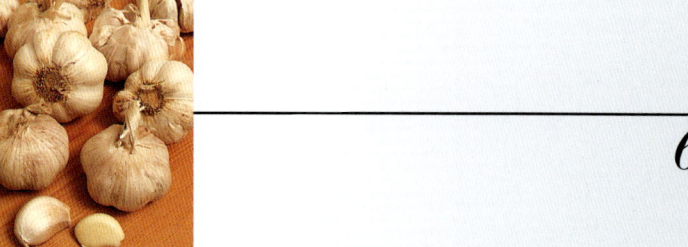

MARCH

8

9

10

11

Garlic

Medicinal uses
Garlic is used to clear catarrh and can help reduce cholesterol levels.

12

A TOUCH OF GARLIC
Rub a crushed clove round the base of a fondue pot to impart a hint of garlic flavor to the ingredients.
This is also ideal for ovenproof porcelain dishes and wooden salad bowls.

13

14

Basil

Basil is a pungently aromatic herb. Originally from Asia, it has become an indispensable ingredient in Italian cooking. Basil is regarded as a sacred plant in India and Greece. The basil plant needs warmth and sun, with protection from wind, frost and scorching. It grows best in well-drained, moist soil. Grow basil near tomato plants as it keeps disease and pests away. Basil also grows well indoors.

Bush, or Greek, basil is a dwarf, compact variety. It is a branched and compact plant. Its leaves have a milder, clove-like flavor.

Basil leaves should be picked when young. They can be dried or frozen (first paint both sides with olive oil), and should be stored in olive oil with salt or dry-packed with salt.

Medicinal uses

- Make a tonic by steeping a few leaves in wine for several days.
- An infusion of basil leaves aids digestion.

Place pots of basil on a windowsill to deter flies.

15

16

17

Basil

18

19

20

21

MARCH

22

Parsley is one of the most nutritious herbs, its roots, stems, leaves and seeds all having beneficial properties. Parsley is high in vitamins A and C and the leaves contain organic iron. It often goes into mixed herbs with thyme, sage and marjoram.

23

24

25

Grow parsley near roses, it improves their health and scent.

26

Parsley

27

28

Parsley

Parsley was consumed in large quantities by the Romans. There are many varieties, all rich in chlorophyll, vitamins and mineral salts.

Parsley thrives in moist, fertile soil in full sun or light shade. It also grows well in a pot or window box.

Once picked, parsley will stay fresh for a few days if kept in a plastic bag in the refrigerator, or if sprinkled with water and wrapped in paper towels.

Culinary uses

- Parsley enhances other flavors, but should be added near the end of cooking.
- Flat-leaf, or Italian parsley, has the most flavor and is best for cooking.
- Finely chop curled parsley and sprinkle over boiled potatoes as a garnish.

Thyme

Thyme is a highly aromatic native of the Mediterranean region. It has powerful antiseptic and preservative properties. Plant thyme in full sun, in light, well-drained alkaline soil. It must be pruned frequently in summer and protected in winter. It can also be grown indoors. Common thyme (Thymus vulgaris) is a woody perennial. It grows up to 12 in/30 cm in height. Its leaves are grey-green, tiny, set in pairs and dotted with scent glands. Thyme is a good complement to lavender.

Thyme

Pick the leaves in summer and preserve them by drying or making thyme vinegar and oil.

Culinary uses

- Make a 'bouquet garni' by mixing thyme with parsley and bay.
- Add fresh, dried or powdered thyme to stocks, stews, marinades, stuffings, sauces and soups.

LES PLANTES MÉDICINALES

Medicinal uses

- Aids digestion of fatty foods.
- Thyme tea helps digestion and hangovers.
- Sweeten thyme with honey for coughs, colds and sore throats.
- Thyme oil reduces cell ageing, and is antiseptic and antifungal.
- Thyme relieves muscular pain and rheumatism, and stimulates the immune system to fight infection.

Caution: Avoid during pregnancy.

Herb

1

2

3

4

5

6

7

Herb Gardens

The culinary and healing properties of herbs have long been recognized, and herb gardens have been cultivated for hundreds of years. Herb gardens vary greatly in size and complexity — from elaborate medieval cloister gardens, sunken gardens, and Tudor and Elizabethan formal gardens to simple, neat gardens with paths of mown grass, paving stones or pebbles. Most herbs are extremely easy to grow and will be happy growing in anything from a small pot to an unused section of the garden. As well as having culinary and medicinal uses, herbs add beauty and fragrance to a garden and can be grown solely for their flowers.

We are a garden walled around,
Chosen and made peculiar ground;
A little spot enclosed by grace,
Out of the world's wide wilderness.
Isaac Watts, 'The Church the Garden of Christ'

APRIL

8

9

10

11
Gardens

12

13

14

Think about the shape or style you want your garden to take. Formal herb gardens are based on patterns and geometric shapes. Informal gardens can be given free rein, with species and colors all mixed together. Even though informal gardens may look unplanned, the best ones are well planned. The plants have to be accessible, so paths are a good idea. Another solution would be to divide the garden up into four sections and put paving stones around the outside and through the middle, making it easy to maintain and providing good accessibility. Most herbs originated in warm Mediterranean areas, growing in sandy, rocky soil. A successful herb garden needs to be well drained and situated in a sunny position. Most herbs grow well in soil that is not too rich and with a light dressing of lime. A little well-rotted animal manure applied sparingly and a little blood and bone helps plants along. Herbs grown in containers should be given half the usual amount of fertilizer used on a herb garden, but they should be fed four times during the year because the fertilizer tends to leach out more easily.

When planting a herb garden it should be kept in mind that some herbs — including mint, thyme, Italian parsley and horseradish — are rampant growers and must be kept in check. Mint is best grown in a disused area of the garden so that it can run riot. If you are creating a formal herb garden, grow perennials to the rear of the bed; this will give you space to plant annuals in the front half of the garden. Herbs can be grown as borders in conjunction with vegetables. Mint and chives or mint and garlic can enhance the appearance of, for example, a cabbage bed and also repel chewing insects.

15

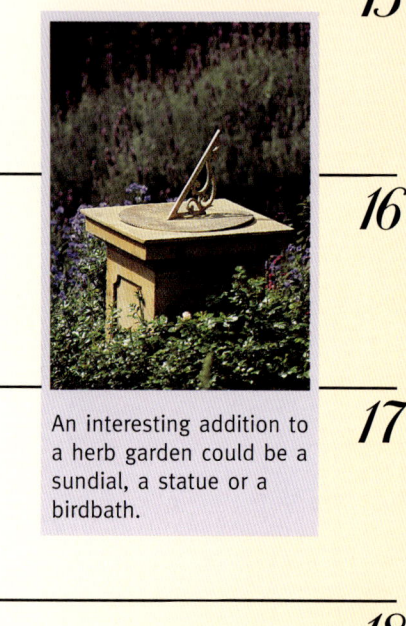

16

17

An interesting addition to a herb garden could be a sundial, a statue or a birdbath.

Comfrey makes an excellent fertilizer for poor soil. Loosely fill a container with comfrey leaves. Add water, cover and ferment for three weeks. Dilute 3 fl oz/85 ml to 18 cups (144 fl oz/4.5 L) of water.

18

Herb

19

20

21

MAINTENANCE TIPS

- Control the growth of invasive herbs such as mints by putting them in pots before planting outside.
- Basil, tarragon and marjoram grow bushier if the growing tip is pinched out (pulled off) first.
- Remove no more than $2/3$ of the leaves and allow time to regrow.
- Prune lavender, rosemary and sage after summer flowering.
- Give herbs a substantial watering when dry rather than a little water more frequently.
- Remove dead or damaged leaves and faded flowers.

APRIL

22

23

24

25

26

Gardens

27

28

Herbs can suit hanging baskets, but their location is important. They dislike high wind and full sun all day. Plants that grow well in hanging baskets include double flowered chamomile, creeping thymes, golden marjoram and pennyroyal. Line the basket with sphagnum moss followed by a layer of black plastic with holes punched in it. Fill the basket half full with compost and position the plants, with the more upright herbs in the middle. Take care not to overcrowd. Fill up the basket with compost and water well. Drain the basket before hanging it.

Herbs are grown easily in containers, as long as they have plenty of sun and air. Make sure you choose a container to suit the plant. If the plant is tall, make sure the container has a base wide enough to prevent it falling over. A collection of containers can be easier to look after than a window box. Make sure the containers have drainage holes, with gravel or broken pots in the bottom of the container to stop the holes clogging up.

Herb Gardens

There's fennel for you, and columbines;
there's rue for you; and here's some for me;
we may call it herb of grace o' Sundays.
O! you must wear your rue with a difference.
William Shakespeare, Hamlet

A strawberry pot is an attractive way of growing a number of herbs together. They are made mainly of terracotta and are easily obtainable. An average size strawberry pot has five or six lipped holes in the sides and one large hole in the top. To plant a strawberry pot with herbs, place one large or several smaller, uneven stones above the drainage hole in the base. Fill the jar with potting mixture to the level of the lowest holes. Plant a herb seedling down through the pot's main open hole, gently manipulating the foliage through one of the side holes with the roots within. Fill the pot with soil level to the next hole and repeat the process as for the first seedling, until the top has been reached. Leave about 1 in/2.5 cm between the last layer of soil and the rim of the pot to allow for watering.

Roses

The Rosa genus contains thousands of varieties, and no one type has been used specifically for culinary and medicinal use. Some varieties of rose are useful for making toiletries and food recipes, but it is most important to choose a rose with plenty of scent. The best ones are the old-fashioned roses, although many of these may have only one flowering period a year.

ROSE POTPOURRI

Mix 8 cups of dried, fragrant rose petals with 1 tbsp each ground allspice, ground cinnamon and ground orris and a few drops of rose oil. Store in a sealed container for 6 weeks before arranging in open bowls or potpourri containers.

Rose scent has perfumed lotions, potpourris, toilet waters and bath oils for centuries. All kinds of toiletries can be made using fresh rose petals.

ROSE LOTION

- 2 cups deep red rose petals, fresh or dried
- 1 cup (8 fl oz/250 ml) spring water
- 1 cup (8 fl oz/250 ml) white wine vinegar
- ½ cup (4 fl oz/125 ml) rosewater

Put the rose petals in a screwtop jar. Boil the water and vinegar, and pour over. Leave for several days, shaking daily. Then add the rosewater and pour into a stoppered bottle. This mild astringent lotion can be dabbed onto the skin after cleansing.

1

2

3

4

Roses

5

6

7

MAY

8

9

10

11

12

13

Roses

14

Queen of Fragrance, lovely Rose,
The Beauties of thy Leaves disclose!

The winter's past, the Tempests fly,
Soft Gales breathe gently thro' the Sky;

The Lark sweet warbling on the Wing
Salutes the gay return of Spring:

The silver Dews, the vernal Show'rs,
Call forth a blooming Waste of Flow'rs;

The joyous Fields, the shady Woods,
Are cloath'd with Green, or swell with Buds;

Then haste thy Beauties to disclose,
Queen of Fragrance, lovely Rose!

William Broome, 'The RoseBud: To the Lady Jane Wharton'

Musk Rose Water

Take two handfuls of your Musk Rose leaves, put them into about a quart of fair water and a quarter pound of sugar, let this stand and steep about half an hour, then take your water and flowers and pour them out of one vessel into another till such time as the water hath taken the scent and taste of the flowers, then set it in a cool place a-cooling and you will find it a most excellent scent-water.
William Rabisha, The Whole Body of Cookery Dissected, *1675*

Rose Water

Rose water, a diluted form of pure rose oil, is an ancient flavoring. Once a favorite in Elizabethan England, rose water is still used in the highly perfumed sweet dishes of India and the Middle East. In Turkey, rose water scents sweetmeats such as Turkish Delight, which is traditionally served with strong coffee. Delicate rose-scented sorbets, ice creams and jellies make an unusual and delicious conclusion to a meal.

Roses

But earthlier happy is the rose distilled,
Than that which withering on the virgin thorn
Grows, lives, and dies, in single blessedness.
William Shakespeare, A Midsummer Night's Dream

MAY

22

23

24

25

26

Roses

27

28

Rose-hip tea is an excellent source of vitamin C, as well as vitamins A, E and B. The hips of wild roses are harvested, dried and shredded. To make rose-hip tea, use one teaspoonful for each cup, pour boiling water over it, allow to infuse, then strain.

Crystallizing Rose Petals

Crystallized rose petals make an ideal dessert decoration. Separate the petals and trim away any white parts. Make sure you work in a dry environment, as they are very sensitive to humidity. Many other edible flowers can also be crystallized, such as violets and borage.

Dissolve 2 oz/60 g gum arabic (or edible gum) in $1^{1}/_{4}$ cups (10 fl oz/310 ml) warmed rose water. Allow to cool. With tweezers, dip each petal into the rose water mixture and coat lightly and evenly. Shake the petal gently to remove excess liquid. Dip the coated petals into sugar and place on greaseproof paper to dry. Store in an airtight container lined with greaseproof paper.

Rose Essential Oil

As the rose is 'queen of all flowers', rose oil has been named the 'queen of essential oils'. The petals of thirty damask roses produce just one drop of precious Rose otto essential oil. Rose oil is probably best loved for its marvellously feminine and sensual fragrance. As the poets attest, it has been the aphrodisiac of the ages. But rose oil is valued as highly for its therapeutic qualities and can be used diluted via face and body masssage, skin care, or vaporisers to treat nervousness, sadness or long-term stress. Refreshing in baths, with a mild tonic affect on sensitive skin, rose oil is generally balancing and an excellent remedy for female disorders as well as digestive maladies.

Rose, on this terrace fifty years ago,
When I was in my June, you in your May,
Two words, 'My Rose' set all your face aglow,
And now that I am white and you are gray,
That blush of fifty years ago, my dear,
Blooms in the past, but close to me today
As this red rose, which on our terrace here
Glows in the blue of fifty miles away.

Alfred, Lord Tennyson (1809–92),
'The Roses on the Terrace'

Roses

Many varieties of rose produce rose hips, the capsules surrounding the seed. Rose hips are generally a lovely, bright, shiny red or orange. Rose hips are very high in vitamin C. Rose hips have been used to make drinks and preserves, and to brighten meals. They are the main ingredient in rose-hip syrup, which can be poured over sweet desserts.

ROSE-HIP JELLY

- 1 lb/450 g cooking apples, quartered and unpeeled
- 2 lb/900 g rose hips, roughly chopped
- 4½ cups (36 fl oz/1.1 L) water
- Juice of 1 lemon
- Granulated sugar

Put the apples and rose hips in a large saucepan and pour water over to just cover. Boil gently for about 1 hour, until fruit is very soft. Pour into a jelly bag or a square of muslin and hang up to drip over a large bowl. Do not press the fruit pulp or the jelly will be cloudy. Leave overnight. Measure out the drained juice and, for every 2¼ cups (19 fl oz/600 ml) of juice, measure 1 lb/450 g of sugar.

Put the juice and the sugar into a saucepan. Heat slowly until the sugar dissolves, then boil rapidly until a set is reached, in about 10 minutes. Skim any foam from the surface, then pour into hot, sterilized and sealable jars. When cool, seal the jars.

'The chamomile shall teach thee patience that rises best when trodden most upon'

Chamomile

The chamomile is an ancient healing herb, and is still used for digestive and stress-related disorders. When crushed, its leaves have a sweet apple smell. The chamomile plant requires full sun and well-drained soil. It makes a fragrant lawn and should be planted 4 to 6 in/10 to 16 cm apart for a fragrant lawn. Chamomile is the 'plant's physician'. It benefits all nearby herbs and plants, particularly cabbages, onions and nasturtiums. Chamomile can also be grown indoors.

German chamomile is an annual with unscented foliage. Its flowers have a strong honey scent and it has coarser leaves than the English chamomile.

Used chamomile tea bags can be placed on the eyelids to reduce eye inflammation and the dark shadows caused by fatigue.

Chamomile

Chamomile can be grown near a failing plant to help it revive. A chamomile infusion can be sprayed on seedlings to prevent mildew.

JUNE

8
Chamomile leaves can be gathered at any time and the flowers should be picked when fully open. Both leaves and flowers should be dried quickly.

9

10

11

Chamomile

12

13

14

CHAMOMILE SHAMPOO
Chamomile shampoo brings out the highlights in blonde hair. Mix 1 tbsp of pure soap flakes, 1 tsp of borax and 1 oz/30 g of powdered chamomile. Add 1 cup (8 fl oz/250 ml) of hot water and beat until you have a thick lather. Wet hair with warm water, add lather amd massage well into the scalp. Rinse and repeat.

Medicinal uses

- The English and German chamomiles have been used for centuries for their medicinal properties. Each has a yellow flower center surrounded by white petals. The centers are rounded and ready to pick when the white ray florets turn black.
- Chamomile is useful for treating skin conditions and irritations.
- Applying a flower compress to eczema and wounds helps to reduce pain and inflammation.

Sage

Sage is strong-flavored and as it can overwhelm other herbs, it is best used on its own in cooking. Sage is also a powerful healing plant. The sage plant requires full sun and light, dry, alkaline soil. Cut sage back after flowering, and prune often. Replace every four to five years. Sage will also grow indoors in a sunny position. Pick leaves just before flowering and dry them slowly to preserve the flavor and to avoid mustiness.

15

Burning sage helps to deodorise cooking smells.

SAGE SHAMPOO

Sage shampoo is best used on dark hair. Pour 6 cups (48 fl oz/1.5 L) boiling water over 1 cup of sage leaves, stir, cover and leave to stand for 2 hours. Strain the liquid through a sieve, pressing to extract all the fragrance. Add 6 tbsp grated castile soap and whisk over a low heat until the soap has dissolved. Cool, bottle and label. Shake the bottle well before use and rinse your hair thoroughly after shampooing.

16

17

18

Sage

19

20

21

When sprinkled on linen, sage helps to discourage insects.

JUNE

22

23

24

Sage

25

In the past, sage leaves were boiled in vinegar then applied as a hot poultice for sprains.

26

27

28

Culinary uses

- Combine sage leaves with onion for poultry stuffing.
- Cook sage with rich, fatty meats such as pork and duck.
- Dried sage is more powerful than fresh — use sparingly.

Medicinal uses

- Sage is a digestive tonic and a stimulant.
- It reduces sweating and soothes sore throats.

Caution: Avoid if you are pregnant or have epilepsy.

Rosemary

Rosemary is an aromatic, strongly flavored herb. It grows best in a sunny and sheltered place, and needs well-drained, alkaline soil. It can also be grown indoors in a sunny position. Pick leaves before flowering and strip them off to store. To release the aroma, crush the leaves before using them.

> There's rosemary, that's for remembrance; pray, love, remember ...
> Willian Shakespeare, Hamlet

Rosemary

Culinary uses

- Add sparingly to a variety of dishes, in particular lamb and pork.
- Use sprigs to infuse slow-cooking. Remove before serving.
- Rosemary makes a delicious herb butter for vegetables.

Medicinal uses

- Rosemary is a stimulant for the nervous system and eases rheumatic pain
- It is also an antiseptic gargle and mouth wash.

> Boyle the leaves in white wine and washe thy face therewith and thy browes and thou shalt have a faire face. Also put the leaves under the bedde and thou shalt be delivered of all evill dreames.
> Smell it oft and it shall keep thee youngly.
> Bancke's Herball, 1525

When making hanging baskets of flowers, it is a good idea to include a herb such as a small rosemary plant. This not only gives you subtle leaf color, but also provides pretty flowers. At the end of the season, the rosemary can planted into the garden to provide fresh aromatic herbs for cooking.

'God Almighty first planted a garden; and, indeed, it is the purest of human pleasures'

Francis Bacon, 'Of Gardens'

Herb Lore

Written records of herbal study date back over 5000 years to the Sumerians. A herbal from China, dating around 2700 BC, lists 365 medicinal plants. Among the earliest successes of herbal medicine are those recorded in the history of Ancient Egypt. Myths throughout the world record both mystical and physical properties of herbs.

YARROW'S ancient background and diverse uses are reflected in the number of descriptive folk names that it has. Among some of yarrow's many common names are staunch-weed, woundwort, nosebleed, and knight's mil-foil, all referring to yarrow's reputation for staunching blood. Because of this ability, this useful medicinal herb was considered an essential part of a British army surgeon's kit until the nineteenth century. Yarrow's botanical name *Achillea* refers to the Greek hero Achilles who, according to legend, treated his soldiers' battle wounds with this herb.

ANGELICA was believed to have been a gift from Michael the Archangel to a monk, as an antidote during a terrible plague in the Middle Ages. This is why the herb was called angelica, the guardian angel. This herb features often in monastery gardens. It has long been associated with magic as a proof against witchcraft.

Herb Lore

BASIL originated in India, where it was regarded as a sacred herb. Some say that the name came from 'basilisk', a mythical serpent-like creature that could kill with a look. For many years the plant was linked with poison. Never give basil as a gift — it is said to represent hatred.

1

2

3

4

5

6

7

JULY

8

9

Herb Lore

10

11

12

13

14

For centuries **BAY** wreaths have been associated with glory. Even today we remember our fallen heroes by laying wreaths made of bay leaves on memorials. The bay laurel's association with glory is reflected in the title 'poet laureate'.

HYSSOP is native to southern Europe, and was well known in the ancient world. It was used for purification rites in Egyptian temples. The Bible refers to hyssop as the herb of cleanliness; the priests used it as a purifying plant to cleanse lepers. The Romans also valued hyssop but as a ceremonial and healing plant. It is believed they introduced the herb wherever they went.

Since ancient times **ROSEMARY** has symbolized fidelity, love, and abiding friendship. It has long been regarded as a preserver of youth. The herb is an effective stimulant and some stories say that it was used to awaken Sleeping Beauty in the fairytale of the same name. In the Middle Ages bunches of rosemary were burned to protect against plague. Rosemary also signifies rememberance and has long been associated with memory stimulation. Old Greek frescoes depict students studying and wearing headbands into which sprigs of rosemary are tucked.

15

16

17

Herb Lore

18

MINT, meaning virtue, takes its name from Menthe, Pluto's beloved. Pluto's wife, Proserpine, metamorphosed Menthe into a herb to keep her from Pluto, and the plant bore her name.

19

20

21

JULY

22

23

24

The **MARIGOLD** was once an emblem of obedience and constancy. Old names for this herb include 'sunflower', 'gold', 'rudde' and 'pot marigold'. The marigold opens and closes with the rising and setting of the sun. Its old Saxon name, *ymbglidegold* means 'that which moves round the sun'. *Calendula,* its Latin name, refers to the belief that in the Roman calendar each plant blooms on the first day of the month. In the twelfth century, people with poor eyesight or persistent headaches were advised to gaze upon the bright marigold to improve their condition.

25

26

TANSY, with its long-lasting flowers, represents immortality. In Greek mythology Zeus ordered Ganymede, cup bearer to the gods, be given tansy for its eternal properties. Traditionally, tansy leaves were finely chopped and added to other ingredients to make 'tansy cakes', which were served on Easter Day as a reminder of the bitter herbs that were eaten at the Feast of the Passover. Tansy is an effective and aromatic insect repellent, and for this reason it was a valued herb in the Middle Ages, being strewn on floors to freshen the air and deter insects.

27

Herb Lore

28

RUE is also known as the Herb of Grace, which refers to the time when bunches of rue were used to sprinkle holy water in the path of the priest as he approached to say High Mass. Rue was also said to defend its wearers against black magic. In Elizabethan times rue was associated with repentance. The expression 'You'll rue the day' refers to an act to be committed that will require repentance afterwards.

29

30

31

Herb Lore

MARJORAM, meaning 'blushes', may have acquired its name from the legend which tells of a youth in the service of the King of Cyprus. One day he accidentally dropped a vial of expensive perfume. Overcome with fear and mortification, the youth lost consciousness and the gods changed him into this herb. In early times, marjoram was used as a strewing herb to gives houses a fresh, clean smell. It was also popular as a sweet bag for the linen cupboard.

'Doubtless God could have made a better berry, but doubtless God never did'
William Butler

Strawberries

Strawberries grow in an extremely wide climatic range and are the one berry fruit that negates the general rule that berries grow well only in cool regions. They like a deep rich soil full of organic matter and do best when heavily fertilized with liquid manure. They can be grown as border plants and, as the flowers and berries are very attractive, they make good decorative plants in their own right.

Strawberries hate weeds, which kill them off. They are best grown on either a straw mulch that is freshened regularly or under black polythene matting, where the young plants are poked through holes pierced in the polythene sheets. If polythene is used, great care must be taken to water the plants regularly, as the water can only penetrate down to the soil through the plant holes. The modern strawberry was developed in the last century as a result of many crosses, including the wild strawberry and the Virginian strawberry. The strawberry symbolized the fruit of righteousness and was depicted in paintings as a fruit of Venus or the Virgin Mary.

Strawberries

The berries themselves are often brought to the Table as a reare service, whereunto claret wine, creame or milke is added with sugar, as every one liketh … and are a good cooling and pleasant dish in the hot Summer season.
John Parkinson, Paradisus, 1629

It is not clear how the strawberry got its name. The most likely explanation is that it came from the Old English word, *streawbridge*, or 'strawed berry', from its appearance of having been strewn on the ground.

AUGUST

8
The French perfumery industry recognized the commercial potential of the scented geranium in the early 19th century, and now Oil of Geranium is an essential oil in aromatherapy.

9
Before the invention of artificial food flavorings, Victorians used scented geranium leaves in the bottom of cake tins to flavor their sponges.

10

11

12

13

Geranium

14

Geranium

Scented geraniums form a group of marvellously aromatic herbs. Originally native to South Africa, they are now widespread throughout many temperate countries. Geraniums have long been appreciated for their hardiness, and they grow well in both tubs and open garden beds. Although scented geraniums can be grown from seed, cuttings are much more likely to be successful. They should be planted as soon as there is no danger of frost. Choose a warm site with well-drained soil. Leaves should be picked during the growing season, for fresh use and for drying. Scented geraniums also make wonderful pot plants and do well as house plants, providing they have plenty of light.

Rose geranium is probably the most familiar and appreciated scented geranium. The tight pink flower heads are very attractive.

When combined in floral arrangements, the foliage of scented geraniums is pleasing both in fragrance and appearance. All the leaves and flowers may be dried for sachets and potpourri. Scented geranium leaves may be added to finger bowls instead of the more usual slice of lemon.

Mint

There are over 600 varieties of mint, and it has been used for medicinal purposes and flavorings for thousands of years. Mint grows best in moist, well-drained alkaline soil that is rich in nutrients. It can also be grown in pots indoors. Mint leaves should be picked just before flowering. To preserve mint leaves, freeze dry or infuse in oil or vinegar.

MINT FACE MASK
Simmer 4 tbsp each finely chopped mint and water for 5 minutes. Remove from the heat and stir in 1 tbsp clear honey, 2 tbsp fine oatmeal and 3 tbsp milk. Cool, then apply evenly over the face, avoiding the eyes. Rest for 30 minutes then rinse.

15

16

17

18

19

Pennyroyal, a variety of mint, has a delightful peppermint fragrance and is excellent with buttered new potatoes.

Mint

20

21

In summer, small sprigs of **peppermint** or **eau-de-Cologne mint** may be individually frozen in ice cube trays in the summer, then dropped into cold drinks.

AUGUST

22

23

24

25

Mint

26

27

28

Culinary uses

- *Mint leaves can be crystallised for decoration.*
- *Use the leaves to make mint sauce, syrups and rich chocolate desserts.*
- *Add fresh spearmint to new potatoes, peas and drinks.*

Medicinal uses

- *Spearmint and peppermint are mildly anaesthetic.*
- *Peppermint leaf tea helps digestion, colds and influenza.*
- *Inhale the vapor of diluted drops of spearmint essential oil to relieve colds.*

Violet

Many poems and songs have been written about the violet. It is a symbol of love, constancy and faithfulness. There are 600 known kinds of violets. Violet was once used as a commercial perfume but, because of the cost of extraction, powdered orris has largely replaced it. The African violet makes a wonderful house plant. It does, however, need the right conditions — moist but not too wet, light and warm but not too sunny.

An infusion of sweet violets, an old remedy for kidney or bladder pain, has strong tonic, antiseptic and purgative qualities.

Violet

VIOLET HONEY

Stir half a cup of washed violet petals into half a jar of honey. Cover and stand the jar on a cloth in a saucepan. Fill with water to the neck of the jar, bring to the boil and simmer for 30 minutes. Remove the jar from the pan and leave to cool. Let stand for seven days. Warm the jar of honey then strain the honey into a clean jar.

SYRUP OF VIOLET

Crush ½ lb/250 g of flower heads in a mortar. Boil 1½ lb/750 g of sugar and 3 fl oz/100 ml of water to make a syrup and when boiling, add the flowers. Bring to the boil five or six times over a very slow fire. Stir with a wooden spoon. Strain and pour into pot or bottle while hot. Another method is to add 1 oz/30 g of glycerine to the syrup and seal in fruit bottles. Pour over ice-cream and puddings for dessert.

'Fair Quiet, have I found thee here,
And Innocence, thy sister dear!'
Andrew Marvell, 'The Garden'

Herbal Teas

Herbal teas, or infusions as they are often called, are made by steeping the fresh or dried leaves, flowers, fruit, stems or seeds of a plant in boiling water for a few minutes. Herbal teas are becoming more and more popular. They can be drunk at any time of the day, either hot or iced. Each herbal tea has different benefits and can assist in overcoming a variety of indispositions. To make a normal strength tea, pour 1 cup (8 fl oz/250 ml) boiling water over 2 heaped teaspoons finely chopped fresh herbs, or 1 heaped teaspoon crumbled dried herb. Cover and sweeten with honey if you wish.

ROSEMARY makes a strongly flavored tea that stimulates the circulation and can help ease migraines.

RASPBERRY LEAF tea is made from dried raspberry leaves and has a reputation for easing childbirth, as well as assisting lactation and hastening convalescence.

DANDELION can reduce acne because it helps the liver remove toxins from the body. Try drinking two cups of dandelion tea per day.

An infusion of **LAVENDER** will soothe and relax, while **ELDERFLOWERS** and **ELDERBERRIES** have long been used to calm the nerves, and reduce insomnia and migraines.

Herbal

1

2

3

4

5

6

7

SEPTEMBER

8

9

10

11
Teas

12

13

14

MINT — with its hundreds of varieties — is valued as an aid to digestion and combines well with other herbs; it is especially refreshing with lime blossom. **PEPPERMINT** tea is the best known of mint teas and relieves indigestion, bronchitis, headaches, coughs and colds.

CHAMOMILE FLOWER tea is one of the best-known herb teas and has a pungent, grassy flavor when infused. This tea is good for the digestive system, calming the nerves and aiding sleep. German chamomile flowers are considered more potent than other varieties.

BORAGE LEAF tea is used as a heart tonic, as a stimulant for the adrenal glands, and as a purifier to the system. Used as a facial steam, a tea made from the leaves and flowers of borage improves dry, sensitive skin.

Try a cup of **LEMONGRASS** tea first thing in the morning — it will wake you up as well as having a tonic effect on your liver. Being rich in vitamin A, lemongrass tea encourages clear, smooth-textured skin.

SAGE LEAF tea has long been favored for promoting longevity, strengthening the memory and restoring acuteness to the senses.

BASIL LEAF tea is good for the lungs and diseases of the kidneys and bladder. It combines well with borage leaf tea. Basil leaves infused in wine and patted onto the face helps to close enlarged pores.

To make **BERGAMOT TEA** pour boiling water on to 2 tsp fresh flowers, stirring well. Cover and leave in a warm place for 10 minutes. Strain the tea and sweeten with a little honey if desired. Serve with a slice of lemon.

Herbal Beauty

FACIAL STEAMS

Facial steaming is a well-known and popular way to achieve fresher, clearer skin, but do not use it if you have thread veins, serious skin problems or a tendency to flush easily. For a herbal facial steam, the herbs or flowers are simmered in water so that the essences and cleansing properties are released. There are various herbal steams, but the basic method of preparation can be followed for

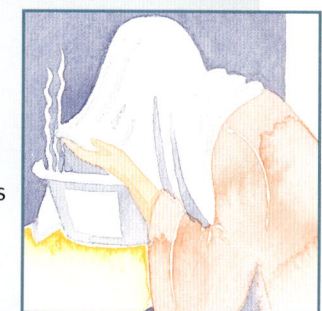

them all. Thoroughly cleanse the skin. Put 2 tablespoons of fresh herb leaves or flowers into 5 cups (40 fl oz/1.25 L) of water in a saucepan and, with the lid on, slowly bring to boiling point. Lower the heat and simmer the liquid for two to three minutes. Turn off the heat, put the saucepan onto a flat surface, and remove the lid. Cover your hair, envelop your head and the saucepan with a towel and lower your face over the the saucepan to within about 8 in/20 cm. Close your eyes for about five minutes for fine skin, and about ten minutes for normal skin.

FACIAL STEAM TO STIMULATE THE SKIN

Chopped peppermint leaves, chopped comfrey leaves, crushed aniseed and rosemary leaves mixed in equal quantities to make 2 tablespoons. Add to 5 cups (40 fl oz/1.25 L) of water and follow the general directions above.

FACIAL STEAM FOR NORMAL TO OILY SKIN

Chopped comfrey leaves and comfrey root, chopped lemongrass, crushed fennel seeds, and crumbled lavender flowers mixed in equal quantities to make 2 tablespoons. Add to 5 cups (40 fl oz/1.25 L) of water and follow the general directions above

FACIAL STEAM TO MOISTURIZE SKIN

Chopped orange peel, whole orange blossoms, chopped comfrey root, and crushed fennel seeds mixed in equal quantities to make 2 tablespoons. Add to 5 cups (40 fl oz/1.25 L) of water and follow the general directions above.

SEPTEMBER

8

9

10

11
Teas

12

13

14

MINT — with its hundreds of varieties — is valued as an aid to digestion and combines well with other herbs; it is especially refreshing with lime blossom. **PEPPERMINT** tea is the best known of mint teas and relieves indigestion, bronchitis, headaches, coughs and colds.

CHAMOMILE FLOWER tea is one of the best-known herb teas and has a pungent, grassy flavor when infused. This tea is good for the digestive system, calming the nerves and aiding sleep. German chamomile flowers are considered more potent than other varieties.

BORAGE LEAF tea is used as a heart tonic, as a stimulant for the adrenal glands, and as a purifier to the system. Used as a facial steam, a tea made from the leaves and flowers of borage improves dry, sensitive skin.

Try a cup of **LEMONGRASS** tea first thing in the morning — it will wake you up as well as having a tonic effect on your liver. Being rich in vitamin A, lemongrass tea encourages clear, smooth-textured skin.

SAGE LEAF tea has long been favored for promoting longevity, strengthening the memory and restoring acuteness to the senses.

BASIL LEAF tea is good for the lungs and diseases of the kidneys and bladder. It combines well with borage leaf tea. Basil leaves infused in wine and patted onto the face helps to close enlarged pores.

To make **BERGAMOT TEA** pour boiling water on to 2 tsp fresh flowers, stirring well. Cover and leave in a warm place for 10 minutes. Strain the tea and sweeten with a little honey if desired. Serve with a slice of lemon.

Herbal Beauty

For thousands of years women have used herbs to prepare cosmetics to care for their skin, hair, eyes and lips and to enhance their natural beauty. The ancient Egyptians and Greeks were highly skilled in the use of herbs and oils for making beauty preparations.

HERBAL BATH

Simply tie up a bunch of your favorite herbs with string, attach them to the hot water tap and let the water run. The scent of the plants will permeate through both the water and the room. Another method is to put some dried herbs in a muslin bag and drop it into the bath.

FENNEL EYE REFRESHER

Using crushed fennel seeds, make a cold tea. Soak cotton wool pads in the tea and put them on your closed eyelids. Leave for about 20 minutes.

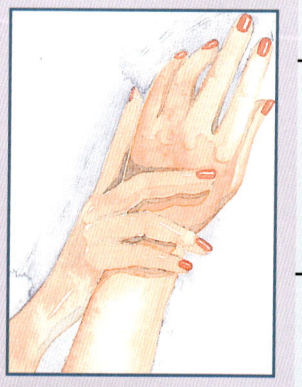

HAND LOTION

Mix 5 parts glycerine to 15 parts rosewater or elderflower water. When using herb water, add a pinch of borax.

Herbal

15

16

17

18

19

20

21

SEPTEMBER

22

23

24

Beauty

25

26

27

28

HAIR RINSES

Use herbal infusions to rinse hair after shampooing.
- To give shine to the hair: rosemary, calendula, nettles, sage, horsetail, parsley.
- To bring out blonde highlights and give sheen: chamomile, calendula, yarrow, mullein flowers.
- To bring out shine and highlights in dark hair: rosemary, nettles, black tea, sage, raspberry leaves, elderberries.

STRAWBERRY MASK

This old beauty treatment can be used to refresh and revitalize the skin. After cleansing the skin, or after a facial steam, cut up and mash enough strawberries to spread all over the face and neck. Keep the eye area clear. Lie down for 20 minutes. Rinse the mask off with warm water, then splash cold water all over the face and neck.

LEMON CLEANSING MILK

Blend together 1/2 small pot of natural yoghurt, 1/2 tablespoon lemon juice, 1 tablespoon safflower or almond oil and use within three days.

HAIR TONIC

Infuse in olive oil: sage, thyme, marjoram, and balm. Allow to stand in bottle in a sunny window for seven or eight days before straining. Rub a little into the scalp before shampooing.

Herbal Beauty

FACIAL STEAMS

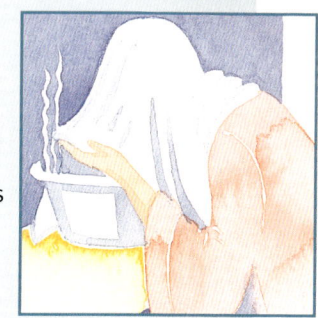

Facial steaming is a well-known and popular way to achieve fresher, clearer skin, but do not use it if you have thread veins, serious skin problems or a tendency to flush easily. For a herbal facial steam, the herbs or flowers are simmered in water so that the essences and cleansing properties are released. There are various herbal steams, but the basic method of preparation can be followed for them all. Thoroughly cleanse the skin. Put 2 tablespoons of fresh herb leaves or flowers into 5 cups (40 fl oz/1.25 L) of water in a saucepan and, with the lid on, slowly bring to boiling point. Lower the heat and simmer the liquid for two to three minutes. Turn off the heat, put the saucepan onto a flat surface, and remove the lid. Cover your hair, envelop your head and the saucepan with a towel and lower your face over the the saucepan to within about 8 in/20 cm. Close your eyes for about five minutes for fine skin, and about ten minutes for normal skin.

FACIAL STEAM TO STIMULATE THE SKIN

Chopped peppermint leaves, chopped comfrey leaves, crushed aniseed and rosemary leaves mixed in equal quantities to make 2 tablespoons. Add to 5 cups (40 fl oz/1.25 L) of water and follow the general directions above.

FACIAL STEAM FOR NORMAL TO OILY SKIN

Chopped comfrey leaves and comfrey root, chopped lemongrass, crushed fennel seeds, and crumbled lavender flowers mixed in equal quantities to make 2 tablespoons. Add to 5 cups (40 fl oz/1.25 L) of water and follow the general directions above

FACIAL STEAM TO MOISTURIZE SKIN

Chopped orange peel, whole orange blossoms, chopped comfrey root, and crushed fennel seeds mixed in equal quantities to make 2 tablespoons. Add to 5 cups (40 fl oz/1.25 L) of water and follow the general directions above.

> "HERE'S FLOWERS FOR YOU;
> HOT LAVENDER, MINTS, SAVORY, MARJORAM"
> *William Shakespeare,* The Winter's Tale

Borage

Borage has an ancient reputation for lifting the spirits and imparting courage.

Freeze borage flowers in ice cubes to make an attractive garnish for drinks.

Borage

Borage is a native of Mediterranean regions and Asia Minor. The Welsh call borage Llanwenlys, or 'herb of gladness'. It is a vivid plant, and borage flowers attract bees to gardens. Borage grows best in an open, sunny position in light, dry and well-drained soil. It is a good idea to plant borage near strawberries, as they stimulate each other's growth. Small borage plants also grow well indoors. Borage flowers look like five-petalled blue stars. They have a prominent black tip in the centre. To remove flower heads, grasp the black stamen tips and gently separate the flowers from their green back. When crushed, the leaves and stem are cucumber scented.

Culinary uses

- Use crystallized borage flowers to decorate cakes.
- Sprinkle the flowers into salads.
- The leaves and flowers are delicious when added to cider, punch, white wine, Pimms, or lemonade.
- The flowers can be candied by dipping them quickly in egg white, then sugar, and drying on wax paper.

OCTOBER

8

Sweet marjoram leaves are used in potpourri.

9

10

Sprigs of marjoram were used to scour wooden furniture and the sweet bags were stored with linen or placed under a pillow to bring a peaceful sleep.

11

Marjoram

12

13

Sweet marjoram was a symbol of happiness, and the Greeks planted this herb on graves as a cheerful farewell to their relatives and friends.

14

All types of marjoram are propagated by root division. The sweet marjoram is an annual, but a perennial in mild climates. It is slow to raise from seed.

Marjoram

Marjoram is indispensable in Mediterranean cooking, and also has valuable medicinal properties.

Culinary uses

- Marjoram goes particularly well with tomato-based sauces.
- Rub on to roasting meat.
- Chop fresh marjoram into salads or butter sauces for fish.
- Add fresh marjoram in the last few minutes of cooking.

Medicinal uses

- Sweet marjoram tea helps colds, headaches, digestive and nervous disorders.

Dill

Dill's flavored leaves and seeds are popular in eastern European cuisine. The name dill comes from the Norse, *dilla*, meaning to lull. Dill water is still a home remedy for wind in babies.

Medicinal uses

Dill has been an important medicinal herb since biblical times. It has excellent digestive properties. A seed infusion helps to provide relief from hiccups, indigestion, stomach cramps and colic.

Culinary uses

- Flavor and garnish meat or fish with finely chopped leaves.
- Use the flowering tops or seed in egg, seafood and potato dishes.
- Dill seed can be sprinkled over bread, pastries and apple pie, and is used in butter or mayonnaise as a spicy sauce for fish.
- Dill is tasty in a Turkish-style salad of yoghurt and cucumber.

DILL BUTTER
Mix dried dill leaf (often called dill weed) and white wine vinegar. Spread on boiled fish, or on cabbage or green beans.

OCTOBER

22

23

Lemon

24

25

26

27

28

LEMON POTPOURRI

Combine 1 cup each of dried lemon verbena and lemon balm leaves, 1 cup each of dried forsythia and chamomile flowers and 1 cup of dried marigold petals. Stir in the thinly pared rind of a lemon and 3 tbsp ground orris. Cover and leave in a warm, dry place for six weeks. Stir in five or six drops of lemon verbena oil to complete.

Lemon

Lemon verbena is a South American plant and was once extensively used in cosmetics. Its leaves have a delicious lemon fragrance. Lemon verbena grows best in light, well-drained, alkaline soil. Although the leaves can be picked at any time, it is at its most fragrant when its flowers begin to bloom. Use fresh leaves to flavor oil and vinegar. When drying the leaves, keep the pieces as large as possible to avoid loss of oil through exposure to air. Dried lemon verbena leaves are ideal in potpourri, linen sachets and herb pillows, they retain their scent for two to three years.

Culinary uses

- Use lemon verbena leaves as a flavoring for drinks, fruit puddings and ice cream.
- Chop the leaves finely or remove them before serving.

Medicinal use

- Lemon verbena tea has a mildly sedative quality and is believed to sooth abdominal discomfort and digestive spasms.
- Lemon verbena can be used to reduce puffiness in eyes. Soak some cotton wool in a leaf infusion, then place over the eyes for 15 minutes.

Dandelion

The dandelion should be grown as an annual to prevent bitterness developing in the plant. Grow it from seed in full sun with a little water — but be careful, it can take over the garden. Dandelions can look attractive growing in containers, especially in window boxes, but the containers will need to be deep to accommodate the long tap root. The dandelion is rarely attacked by either pest or disease.

The traditional day for picking the first dandelions is St George's Day on April 23.

29

30

Dandelion

31

Culinary Uses

Both the leaves and root have long been eaten as a highly nutritious salad, considered to be a blood cleanser owing to its diuretic and digestive qualities. Dandelion flowers make an excellent country wine and the roots provide, when dried, chopped and roasted, the best known coffee substitute. The leaves should be picked as required to use fresh and to make wine, the flowers should be picked as soon as they are fully open. Dig up roots in autumn for drying.

"Beauty is the lover's gift"
William Congreve, The Way of the World

Herbal Gifts

The possibilities of herbs are unlimited. Whether you simply tie a bunch of lavender with a pretty ribbon, create an elegant garland, or blend a jar of fragrant bath herbs, a pleasing touch can be added to any room.

Herbal

To dry herbs and flowers succesfully, they must be picked at their peak. Herbs are usually at their best after a rather dry summer. Once a plant has reached full maturity, harvesting must be done or the plant will die back and its valuable oils will return to the roots. Cutting should be done on a dry day after the dew has left the plants and before its natural oils have been drawn out by the sun. Once cut, herbs should be left to dry for an hour or so, but should not be overexposed to sunlight. Gather the herbs into bunches and tie them together with string or use a rubber band. Suspend them from the ceiling of a dry shed, attic or ceiling beam, or spread them out on shelves or trays (not stone or iron). Most herbs will dry within a week. The herbs and flowers are dry when they are crisp to the touch. Strip the leaves or flowers from the stalks, remove soil and chaff, and store in clearly labelled, clean, airtight jars.

LAVENDER HANGERS

This pretty clothes hanger has been stuffed with dried lavender. A collection of small lavender hangers is a lovely gift for a new baby, and the fragrance will last for years.

HERBAL PILLOWS

Hand-made herbal pillows or sachets are ideal gifts and are easy to make. Use material such as muslin to create different-shaped pillows and decorate them with lace or embroidery. Fill them with a fragrant mixture of 4 tsp of dried lavender flowers and dried rosemary leaves, 20 lightly crushed cloves and 1 tsp powdered dried orange rind.

NOVEMBER

8

9

PRESSED HERBS

You can use pressed and dried herbs and flowers to make bookmarks, greeting cards and pictures. You will need a soft paintbrush, rubber-based glue, pressed petals and leaves. Sketch your design then position the herbs. Lift them and apply some glue with a cocktail stick. Let one layer dry before adding the next. Cover designs with a sheet of glass or board and weigh down with books overnight so that the herbs dry flat.

10

Gifts

11

CHRISTMAS GARLANDS

With its fine needles and pine-like smell, rosemary, the symbol of friendship, is an obvious choice of herbs for Christmas. Bind branches of rosemary to form a garland and decorate it with white roses; this herbal garland can be used to festoon windows and doors. Herbs are also wonderful in Christmas wreaths — add juniper, bay, myrtle and winterberry to the wreath on the front door.

12

13

14

FLOWER SACHETS

Sachets of lavender and lemon verbena have been used for centuries to perfume drawers and cupboards and to keep moths and silver fish at bay. Almost any fine material may be used to make flower sachets. Once sewn, turn the bags inside out so that the stitching is on the inside. When the bag has been filled, draw the top in and fasten a strip of ribbon around the top. Finish with a small bow.

Herbal

Tussie-mussie

The word 'tussie-mussie' is an old fashioned name for little posies of aromatic herbs and flowers. In medieval England men and women carried tussie-mussies made from herbs such as rosemary and thyme to mask unpleasant odors and to help protect them from the plague. It was believed that tussie-mussies prevented infection by warding off evil aromas. A herb posy is particularly suitable for the sick room, as the fragrance of assorted herbs adds a pleasant cleansing aroma.

Glass jars filled with candied violets or rose petals make delicious and attractive gifts. Do not mix the sweets, as the flavors will intermingle. Decorate the jars with a length of ribbon tied into a bow and a label describing the contents.

15

16

17

18

19

20

21

NOVEMBER

Herb Vinegars

Herb vinegars make delightful, unusual and useful gifts. The vinegar may be flavored with various herbs or with a combination of herbs. Tarragon, rosemary, basil, thyme, marjoram, garlic, dill and mint all make strong flavored vinegars when used on their own. Combine parsley and fennel or parsley and garlic for a tasty vinegar. Making herb vinegars is easy. Pick and wash the herbs, then dry them on absorbent paper. Pack the leaves into clean bottles or jars with lids and fill with white wine vinegar, replacing the lids firmly. Stand the infusing vinegars on a sunny windowsill for about two weeks. If the herbs lose their color after soaking in the vinegar, strain the vinegar into a clean bottle and put in a fresh, washed sprig of the herb. This will add flavor as well as improve the appearance.

22

23

24

25

Gifts

26

CANDIED VIOLETS

Choose perfect flowers, remove all green, wash them and pat dry with paper towels. Using a toothpick, dip each violet first into an egg-white, which has been beaten until foamy, and then into caster sugar, coating thoroughly. Place on greaseproof paper to dry. Store in an airtight container.

27

28

Herbal Gifts

Potpourri

- 3 cups assorted perfumed flower petals and leaves
- 1 cup sea salt
- ½ tablespoon ground cloves
- ½ tablespoon ground allspice
- ½ cup orris root powder
- 6 drops rose oil

Gather flowers and leaves during dry weather early in the day, before the sun has become too hot. Spread the flowers and leaves out to dry in a shady, well-aired place.

In a large deep bowl place alternate layers of petals and salt, filling it to about two-thirds full. Stand the bowl in a dry, airy place for ten days. The petals, the basis of the potpourri, will be ready when they have caked together. Break apart the caked petals and add the remaining dry ingredients. Place in an airtight container and store for six weeks. During this time, stir the mixture frequently. At the end of six weeks, add the rose oil and seal the container and leave for a further two weeks. To store, divide into smaller airtight containers. The potpourri mixture is now ready to be placed in decorative bowls.

'Blowing sweet o'er each enclosure,
Grateful offerings of perfume'

Christopher Smart, Hymns and Spiritual Songs

Aromatherapy

The pleasure of using the pure essences of fragrant plants has been recognized for centuries. Since ancient times essential oils have been thought to benefit the body, mind and emotions. In the Middle Ages, monks cultivated herbs and discovered many of their restorative properties. They were among the first to distil precious plant essences and use them to administer to patients. These concentrated pure plant extracts, valued for their fragrance and their therapeautic value, are termed essential oils. The use of such oils is known as aromatherapy. Harness the therapeutic and beneficial properties of oils to enhance every aspect of your health and well-being. You can use essential oils in many ways and most methods do not require any special equipment.

FLOWER OILS

Although it is easier to buy flower oils than to make them yourself, it is fun to make your own. Pick 10 large cupfuls of fragrant petals. Heat $1\frac{1}{4}$ cups (19 fl oz/300 ml) almond oil in the top of a double boiler and stir in 2 cups of petals. Cover tightly and leave on a low heat for 2 hours. Strain, reserving the flowers. Add fresh flowers and repeat until you have used all the flowers. Pour the oil and all the flowers into a pan and simmer over a low heat for 1 hour or until the flowers are dry. Press the oil through muslin or a sieve. Stir in 1 tsp of liquid storax and tincture benzoin, bottle, seal, label and store in a dry, dark place.

1

2

3

4

5

Aromatherapy

6

7

DECEMBER

8

9

10

11

12

13

14

RELAXING BATH RECIPE
- 2 drops lavender
- 2 drops bergamot
- 2 drops cedarwood

This mix of oils is particularly calming, balancing and uplifting.

AROMATHERAPY MASSAGE

Essential oils penetrate the skin very quickly to reach the bloodstream, so they are perfect when used with massage therapy. Because essential oils are highly concentrated they are best diluted in base carrier oils to enhance their penetration power. Use only 100% pure unrefined cold pressed vegetable, nut or seed oils, not mineral oils. For massage the usual proportion is about 23 drops essential oils to 1 teaspoon (5 ml) carrier oil. You need only about a teaspoonful for each massage. Where a stronger blend is indicated for healing, use about 15 drops in 1 oz (30 ml).

MASSAGE BASE CARRIER OIL BLEND

To make 2 oz (50 mls)
- 1½ tbsps (30 mls) sweet almond or grapeseed oil
- 1 tsp (5 mls) jojoba oil
- 1 tsp (5 mls) avocado oil
- 1 tsp (5 mls) wheatgerm oil

Aromatherapy Bath

The aromabath is one of the easiest and most delightful ways to indulge oneself. The therapeutic benefits of an aromabath are twofold: oils are absorbed through the skin and enter the circulatory system, and their fragrance is inhaled through the olfactory system. Aromabaths can be refreshing, relaxing or detoxifying, depending on the oil you use. Fill the bath with hand-hot water, then add the essential oils. Disperse the oils well before stepping into the water. Use about 6 to 12 drops of essential oil for each bath. Alternatively, rub on some blended massage oil before getting into a bath or shower.

Try a little patchouli or cedarwood on a cotton ball to protect clothes from moths. Use sparingly or the smell may be too heavy.

Personalized Perfumes

The sense of smell is the most direct trigger of our emotions. Certain smells inspire romance, others just make us feel good. There is nothing nicer than to surround oneself with a pleasing aroma. Whether your preference is for the heavy sweet oils or the light and fresh, experiment until you find a scent that suits you.

FLOWERY Bergamot 8 drops, geranium 8 drops, neroli 4 drops

ROMANTIC Rose 4 drops, sandalwood 12 drops, geranium 2 drops, rosewood 2 drops

SPICY Sandalwood 10 drops, cedarwood 5 drops, rosewood 4 drops, lemongrass 1 drop

SUBTLE For a subtle blend, in 2 teaspoons (10 ml) jojoba oil add 2 drops essential oils.

CALMING Geranium 1 drop, lavender 1 drop

REFRESHING Geranium 1 drop, orange 1 drop

UPLIFTING Rosewood 1 drop, clary sage 1 drop

DECEMBER

22

23

24

Aromatherapy

25

To give a fresh aroma to towels add 1 drop of lemon in the rinse water or sprinkle a drop in the clothes dryer.

26

27

28

To perfume your lingerie add 1 drop of chosen essential oil to the final rinse water of the washing. Try rose, geranium jasmine, neroli or ylang ylang. Take care to ensure the oil is well dispersed in the water and does not directly touch the lingerie.

FOOTBATHS

Add four to eight drops of essential oil to a bowl of warm to hot water. Soak for about 15 minutes to refresh the feet.

Aromatherapy

A drop of lavender in the final rinse of a wash cycle will impart a lingering restful aroma to sheets and bed linen.

Essential Effects

Basil	uplifting, refreshing, clarifying, aids concentration
Bergamot	refreshing, uplifting
Chamomile	refreshing, relaxing, calming, soothing, balancing
Clary sage	warming, relaxing, uplifting, calming, euphoric
Fennel	carminative, eases wind and indigestion
Geranium	refreshing, relaxing, balancing, harmonizing
Hyssop	decongestant
Jasmine	relaxing, soothing, confidence building
Juniper	refreshing, stimulating, relaxing, diuretic
Lavender	refreshing, relaxing, therapeutic, calming, soothing
Lemon	refreshing, stimulating, uplifting, motivating
Lemongrass	toning, refreshing, fortifying
Marjoram	warming, fortifying, sedating
Orange	refreshing, relaxing
Patchouli	relaxing, enhancing to sensuality
Peppermint	cooling, refreshing, head clearing
Pine	refreshing, antiseptic, invigorating, stimulating
Rose	relaxing, soothing, sensual, confidence building
Rosemary	invigorating, refreshing, stimulating, clarifying
Thyme	antiseptic, refreshing, strengthening to immune system
Ylang ylang	relaxing, soothing, enhancing to sensuality

ASTROLOGICAL HERBS

TABLE OF ASTROLOGICAL CORRESPONDENCES

STAR SIGNS	PLANETS	ELEMENTS	HERBS
Aries	Mars	Fire	Chilli, marjoram
Taurus	Venus	Earth	Cumin, lovage
Gemini	Mercury	Air	Meadowsweet
Cancer	Moon	Water	Honeysuckle
Leo	Sun	Fire	St John's Wort
Virgo	Mercury	Earth	Lavender
Libra	Venus	Air	Rose geranium
Scorpio	Mars	Water	Basil
Sagittarius	Jupiter	Fire	Dandelion
Capricorn	Saturn	Earth	Comfrey
Aquarius	Uranus	Air	Star anise
Pisces	Neptune	Water	Hemp

Picture Credits

The Bridgeman Art Library, London/New York

Cover (front and back) The Herb Garden, 1991 (w/c) by Colin Newman (b.1923), John Noott Galleries, Broadway, Worcestershire, UK. **10** The March Marigold, c.1870 by Sir Edward Burne-Jones (1833–98), Piccadilly Gallery, London, UK. **15** The Art of the Apothecary, Latin (manuscript), Apuleius Dioscorides, Eton College, Windsor, UK. **17** Roy 14 E VI f.157, Man teaching a rustic in a herb garden, executed for Edward IV, Bruges, Rustican du Cultivement des Terres, (1473–83), British Library, London, UK. **18** Sloane 1975 f.44, Representations of Medicinal Plants, illuminated copy of the Greek Herbal of Pseudo-Apuleius, Latin, c.1200, British Library, London, UK. **25** Herb Garden at Noon by Timothy Easton (living artist), Private Collection. **26** Topiary Herb Garden by Derold Page (living artist), Private Collection. **41** Ms Nat 1673 f.34, Two women picking sage, 15th century, Bibliotheque Nationale, Paris, France. **45** Picking Flowers, 1881 by Winslow Homer (1836–1910), Private Collection. **46** Spring, 1595 by Lucas van Valkenborch (c.1535–1597), Christie's Images. **48** The Convent Garden Pig by Ditz (living artist), Private Collection. **55** Sunday Afternoon, Ladies in a Garden, c.1890 by English School (19th century), Gavin Graham Gallery, London, UK.

International Photographic Library, Sydney

pp 16 (bottom), 19 (main), 20 (bottom), 22 (top), 23 (bottom), 27, 37 (main), 43 (main), 49 (main), 60, 61 (main & inset), 62, 66 (bottom), 67 (main)

Image Bank, Sydney

pp 19 (inset), 20 (top), 21, 29 (bottom), 31 (main), 49 (inset), 73 (main)

The publishers would like to thank the above for their cooperation in providing pictures for use in this publication. Full effort has been made to locate the copyright owners of images and quotations within this book; we apologize for any omissions which will be rectified in future editions.

This book is intended to give general information only and is not a substitute for professional and medical advice. Consult your health care provider before adopting any of the information contained in this book. The publisher, author, and distributor expressly disclaim all liability to any person arising directly or indirectly from the use of, or for any errors or omissions in, the information in this book. The adoption and application of the information in this book is at the reader's discretion and is his or her sole responsibility.

Published by Lansdowne Publishing Pty Ltd
Level 1, 18 Argyle Street, Sydney NSW 2000, Australia

First published in 1998

© Copyright Lansdowne Publishing Pty Ltd

Publisher: Deborah Nixon
Production Manager: Sally Stokes
Project Coordinator: Kate Merrifield
Designer: Stephanie Doyle
Illustrator: Sue Ninham

ISBN 1 86302 639 8

Set in Cochin and Meta on QuarkXPress
Printed by Tien Wah Press (Pte) Ltd in Singapore

All rights reserved. No part of this publication may be reproduced, stored in a retrieval system, or transmitted in any form, or by any means, electronic, mechanical, photocopying, recording, or otherwise, without the prior written permission of the publisher.